Liar Liar Pants On Fire

How Fi Grow Yuh Pickney Book 2

Written By Catherine Alexander-McDaniel
Illustrated By Krystal Ball
Contributions By Zunammie Keren

Mel

- whose friendship has helped to shape me and keep me in shape.

All my love,
For you, Savannah and Harrison

A Note to Parents/Guardians/Teachers

This series is a plea for us all to do our part in ensuring that we are good examples for children to follow.

As a mother of 2 boys, I was inspired to write these books as I noticed that more and more children lack basic manners and respect. It is my view that our 'village' is failing us. Because of our busy lives, we depend on schools to protect and teach them what should be reinforced and practised in the home. We don't spend the time monitoring what our children are exposed to from the TV, social media and the Internet. We need to sit and explain our religious beliefs and core values and pray for them daily.

These books are for us just as much as they are for the children. Please read together to spark a discussion on core values. Let us also examine ourselves. 'Do as I say and not as I do' cannot be the answer.

We cannot continue to allow our values and morals to be depleted which steer our children to add to the breakdown of our beautiful country, Jamaica.

Let us fight for our children. They are worth it, are they not?

Liar Liar Pants On Fire

Savannah was putting away the laundry when she heard a knock on the door.

Her Uncle Mark came running from the back room.

'Tell them I'm not here!' he said in a hurried whisper.

'But you ARE here' replied Savannah.

'Likkle girl, don't cause mi any problems! Tell dem seh mi nuh deh yah!'

Savannah wasn't sure how her uncle knew who was at the front door but she certainly didn't want to cause any problems for the him as he is the one who takes care of her grandma and herself.

But then, she had always been told not to lie. She remembered when she told her friend Sebastian from school that she had not taken his mango. The truth was, that she had been so hungry that day after not having lunch. When Grandma and Uncle Mark found out, they scolded her and she had to tell Sebastian the truth and apologize.

Even though confused, Savannah figured she better be obedient and went to the door. She slowly opened it as Mr. Brown, the landlord, stood on the front step looking annoyed.

'How yuh do Savannah? Where is your uncle? Is he home?' He asked.

'He's ....um....not here now....um.... Mr. Brown.' Savannah stuttered nervously.

Mr. Brown sighed, 'Did he leave anything for me to collect? Like an envelope?'

Savannah was clearly not prepared for that question as she blurted out 'Oh let me go ask him!'

She quickly realized what she did as Mr. Brown's eyes opened wide. Savannah put her hand over her mouth as Uncle Mark sheepishly came out from the hallway closet.

Just then, Grandma walked up the path and came up behind Mr. Brown.

'Yes Mr. Brown?' Grandma said as she looked at him strangely. 'Not used to seeing you around so late in the month. What happen?'

Mr. Brown seemed cross and replied, 'What happen is yuh son hiding me out for the rent money and mekking poor little Savannah lie for him! Telling her to tell me he's not here!'

'Is that so Mark?' Grandma narrowed her eyes.

Uncle Mark was finding it hard to explain. He knew he was wrong and now he was going to have to make it right.

'I know, I know....' he sighed.

'Savannah your uncle set a bad example for you today. I should never ever tell you to lie, for me or anyone else.' He hung his head.

'I hope I didn't confuse you, I was trying to avoid a problem and not face it with honesty as I should.'

Savannah nodded and was relieved that Grandma had showed up when she did!

'

'And Mr. Brown,' he continued 'I should not have been hiding from you. I should have just been honest and told you I didn't have the full amount for the rent this month.'

Grandma shook her head 'Let this be a lesson for us today. A child learns by example. Of course we all make mistakes but we have to be more aware of the confusion we cause when we don't practice what we preach!'

'I agree with you Grandma, well said. Come Mark, mek mi and yuh go reason about this like two big people. I'm sure we can work something out.' Mr. Brown replied as he lead the way inside the house.

Grandma took Savannah by the hand and stroked her hair.

'You are a good girl. None of us are perfect and we make mistakes. I always want you to feel as if you can ask me to explain anything you are uncomfortable with and we will work it out ... together.'

'Thanks Grandma, I love that you are here to guide me.' she said as she squeezed her grandma with a tight hug. 'Let's go finish up the laundry!'

The End

Nuh hide yuh tick an lick a man

(be honest from the beginning when dealing with others)

Thank You for reading!

How Fi Grow Yuh Pickney Book 2
Liar Liar Pants On Fire

The Author

Catherine was born in Montreal and raised in Jamaica since age 7. She is a sales professional and the mother of 2 boys - Joshua 11 and Jacob 7.This is her first book series intended to revive values and bring more awareness to our own actions.

The Illustrator

Krystal Ball is a Jamaican artist who officially entered the international art scene after winning the Pan American Health Organization's Centennial Poster Competition at the tender age of 10 years old. She has continued to practice art throughout her life after returning from her studies in Philadelphia to reside in Jamaica where she is currently studying Chemistry and is an art instructor.

The Contributor

Zunammie Keren is a Jamaican freelancer writer. She writes books, articles and other web content. Zunammie enjoys reading, writing and spending time at the beach with her husband and their 3 sons.

How Fi Grow Yuh Pickney Series